FINGERPICKING
CLASSICAL

ISBN 978-0-634-06914-7

Visit Hal Leonard Online at www.halleonard.com

HAL•LEONARD®
CORPORATION

7777 W. BLUEMOUND RD. P.O. BOX 13819 MILWAUKEE, WI 53213

INTRODUCTION TO FINGERSTYLE GUITAR

Fingerstyle (a.k.a. fingerpicking) is a guitar technique that means you literally pick the strings with your right-hand fingers and thumb. This contrasts with the conventional technique of strumming and playing single notes with a pick (a.k.a. flatpicking). For fingerpicking, you can use any type of guitar: acoustic steel-string, nylon-string classical, or electric.

THE RIGHT HAND

The most common right-hand position is shown here.

Use a high wrist; arch your palm as if you were holding a ping-pong ball. Keep the thumb outside and away from the fingers, and let the fingers do the work rather than lifting your whole hand.

The thumb generally plucks the bottom strings with downstrokes on the left side of the thumb and thumbnail. The other fingers pluck the higher strings using upstrokes with the fleshy tip of the fingers and fingernails. The thumb and fingers should pluck one string per stroke and not brush over several strings.

Another picking option you may choose to use is called hybrid picking (a.k.a. plectrum-style fingerpicking). Here, the pick is usually held between the thumb and first finger, and the three remaining fingers are assigned to pluck the higher strings.

THE LEFT HAND

The left-hand fingers are numbered 1 through 4.

Be sure to keep your fingers arched, with each joint bent; if they flatten out across the strings, they will deaden the sound hen you fingerpick. As a general rule, let the strings ring as long as possible when playing fingerstyle.

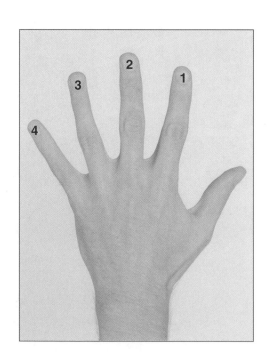

Ave Maria

By Franz Schubert

Drop D tuning:
(low to high) D-A-D-G-B-E

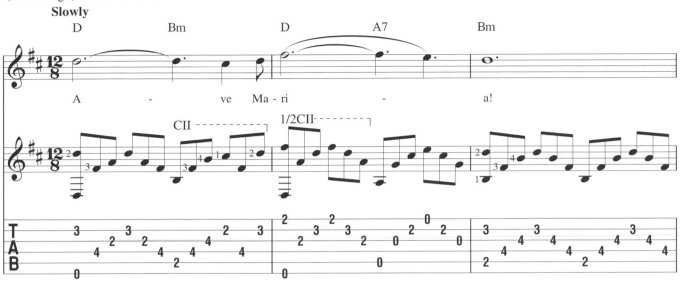

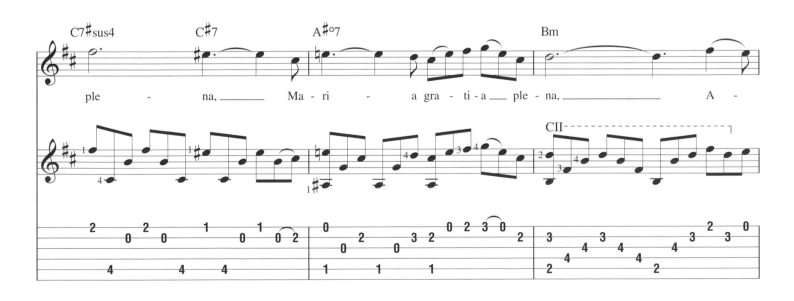

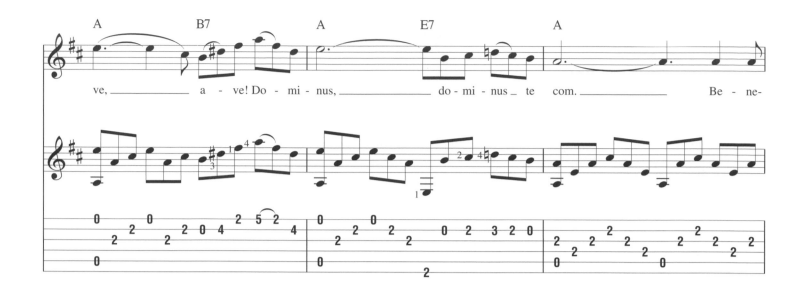

ve, _____ a - ve! Do - mi - nus, _____ do - mi - nus _ te com. _____ Be - ne-

dic - ta tu in mu - li - e - re - bus, _____ et be - ne - dic -

tus, _____ et be - ne - dic - tus, frue - tus ven - tris, _____ ven - tris

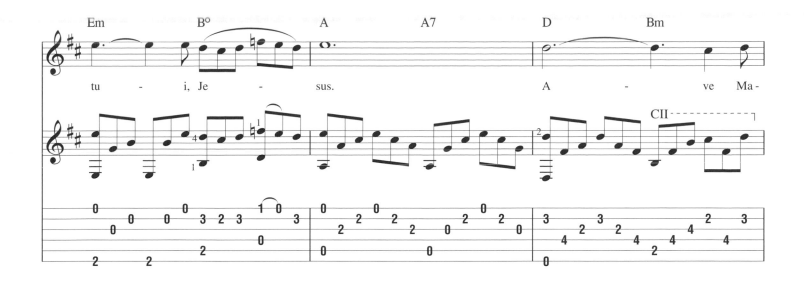

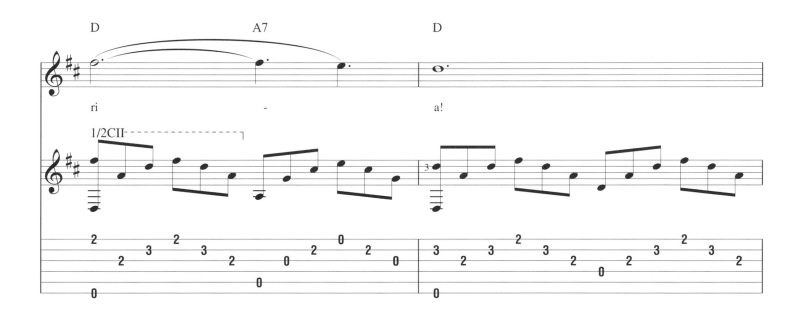

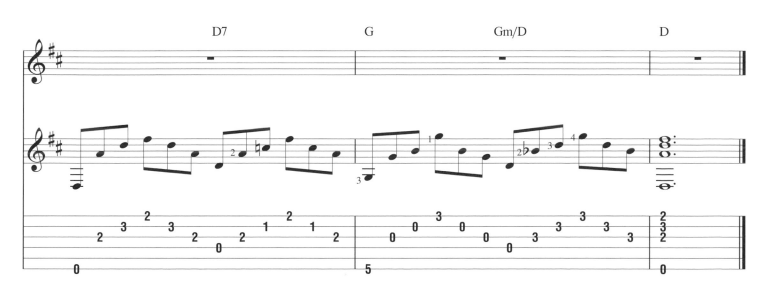

Bourée in E Minor
(Lute Suite #1)

By Johann Sebastian Bach

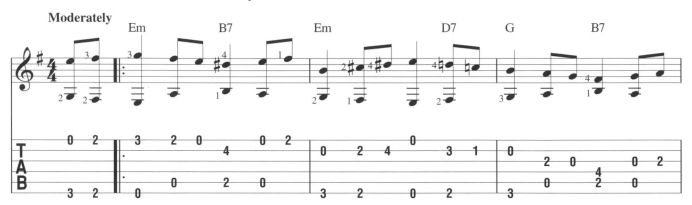

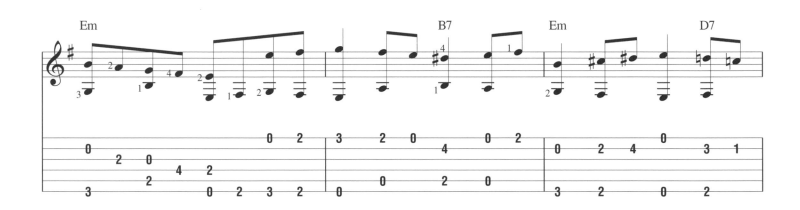

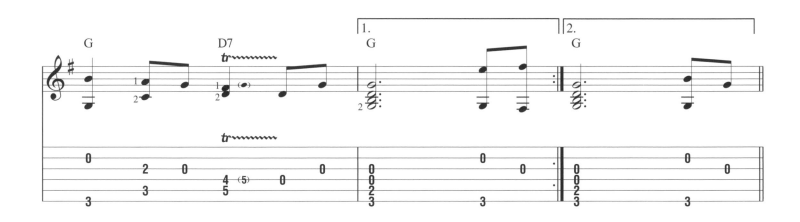

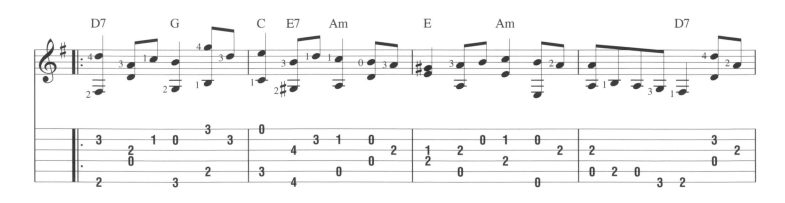

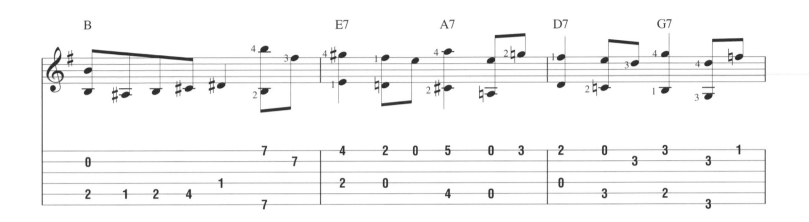

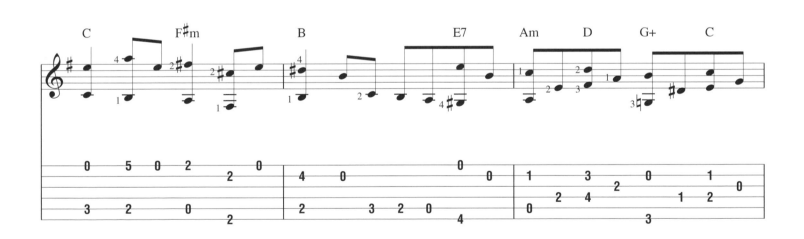

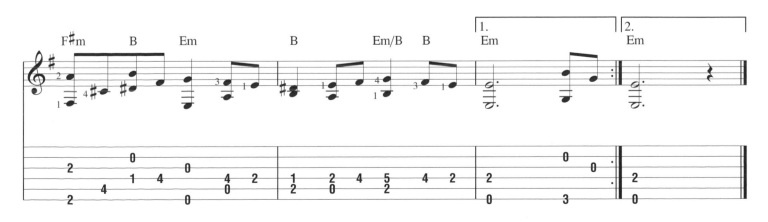

Can Can

from ORPHEUS IN THE UNDERWORLD

By Jacques Offenbach

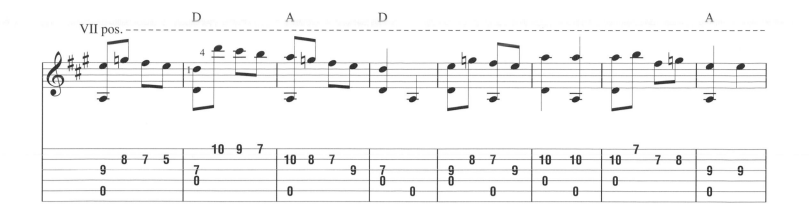

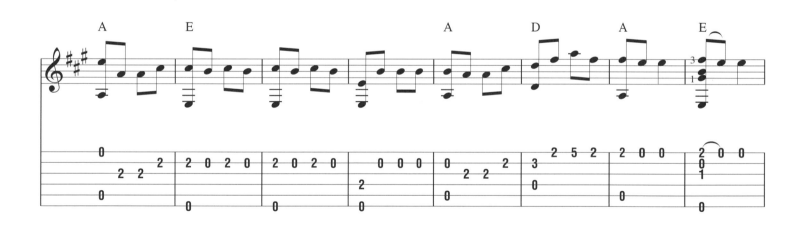

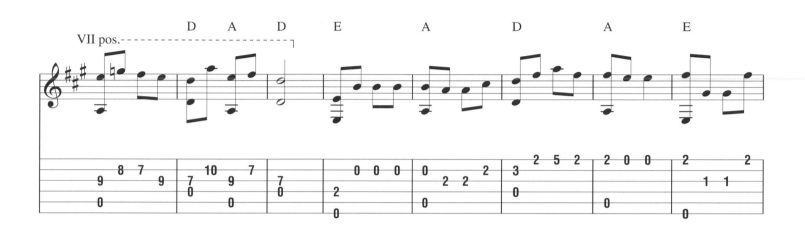

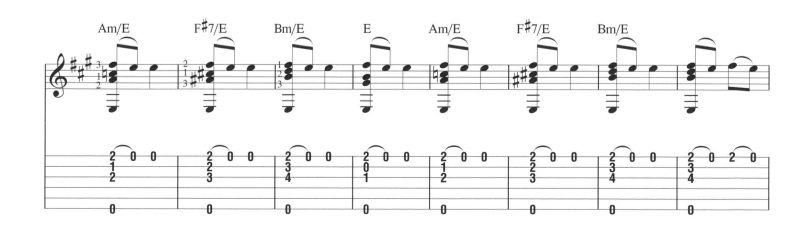

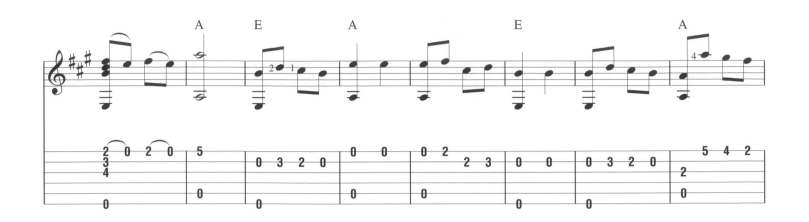

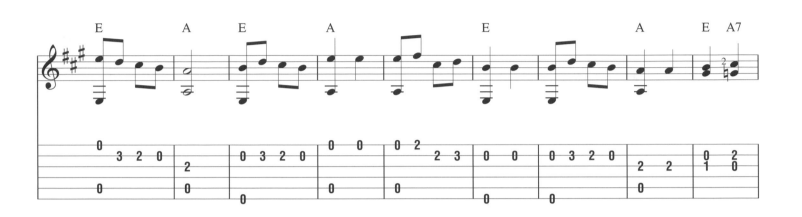

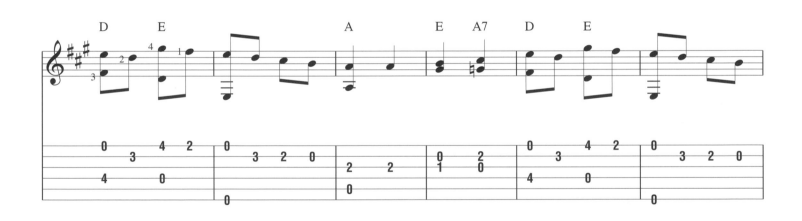

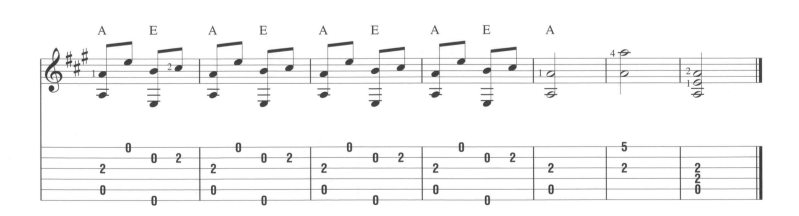

Canon in D

By Johann Pachelbel

*Capo II

Moderately

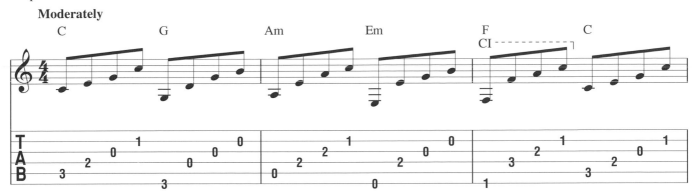

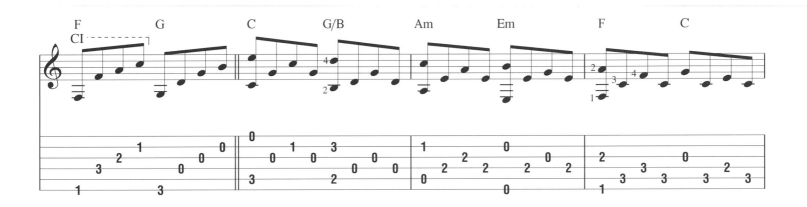

*This arrangement in C major for playability.
To play in D major, capo 2nd fret.

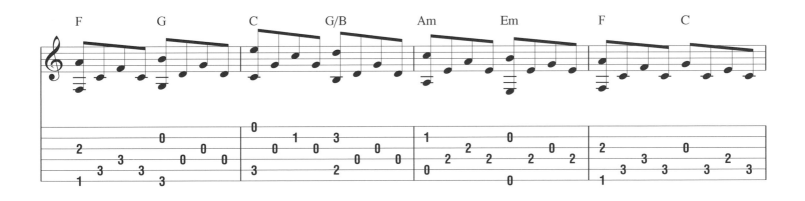

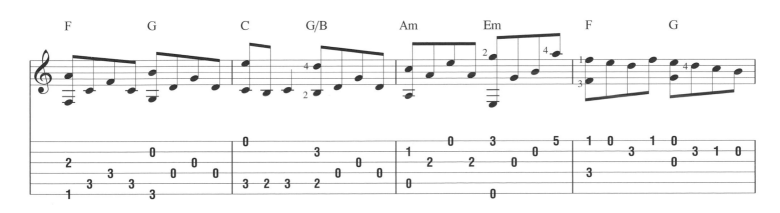

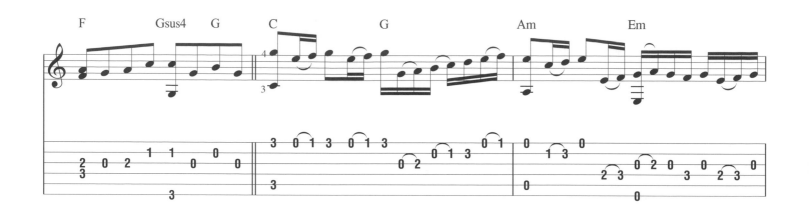

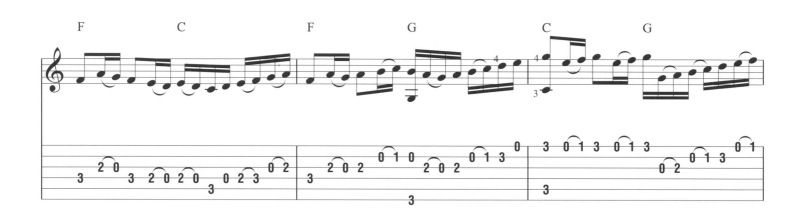

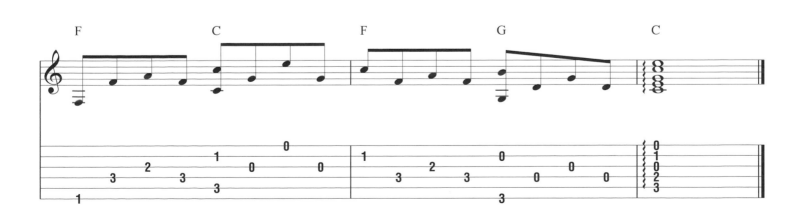

Eine Kleine Nachtmusik

By W. A. Mozart

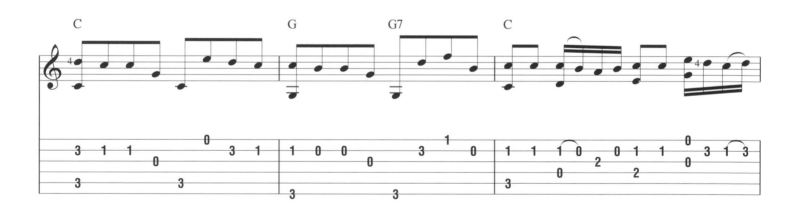

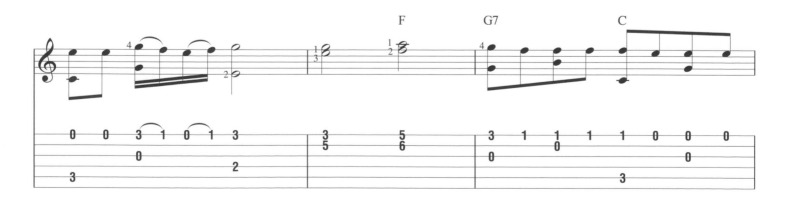

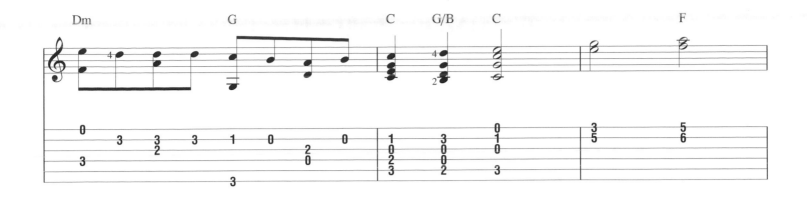

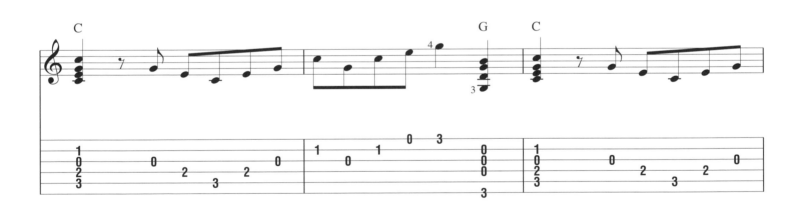

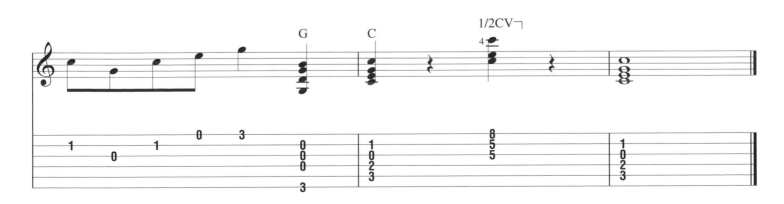

15

Emperor Waltz

By Johann Strauss, Jr.

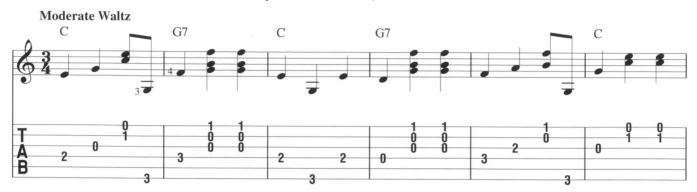

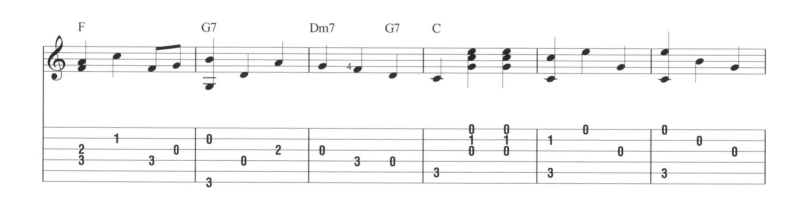

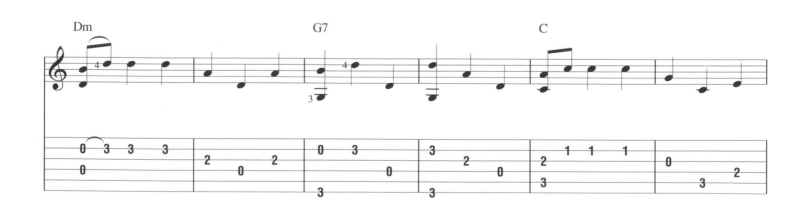

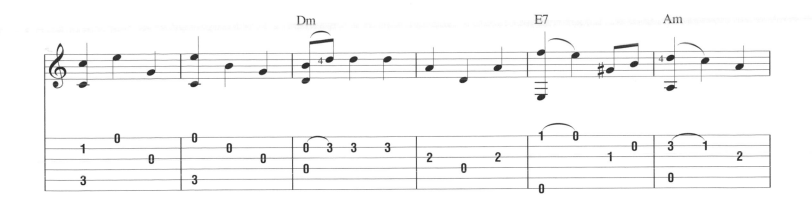

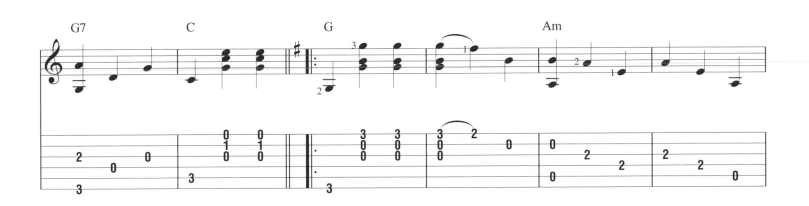

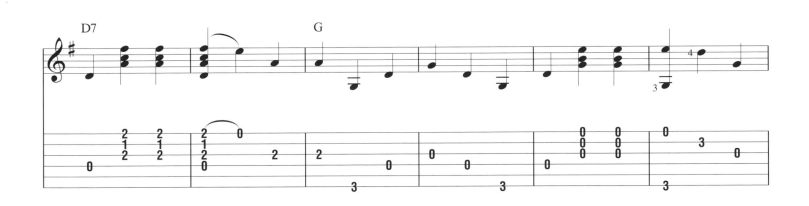

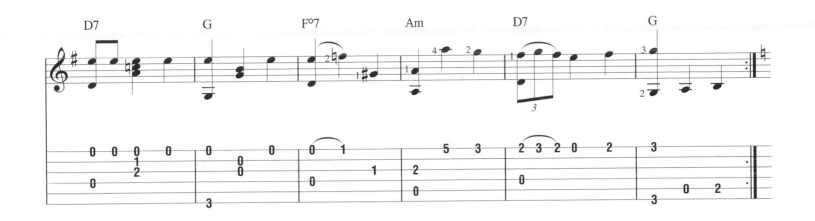

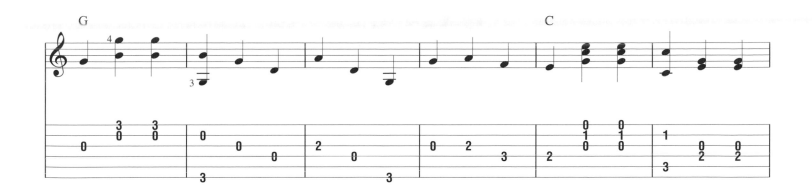

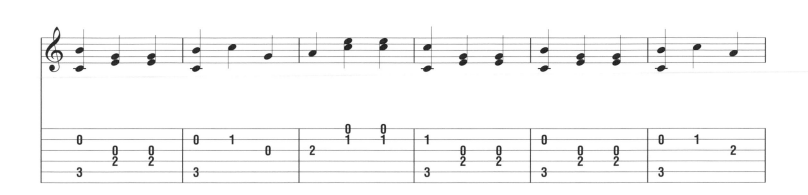

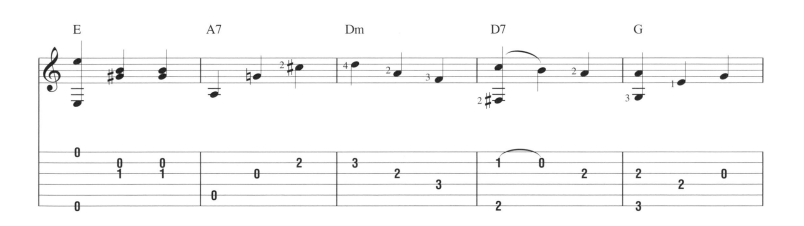

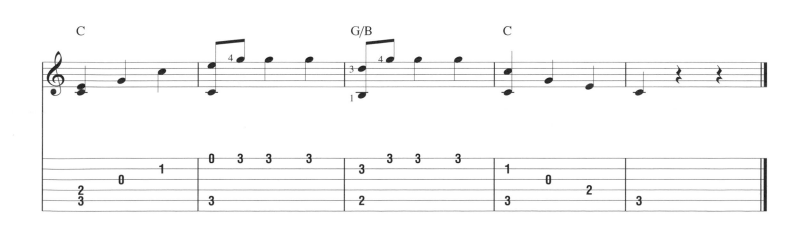

Für Elise

By Ludwig van Beethoven

Habanera

from CARMEN

By Georges Bizet

Drop D tuning:
(low to high) D-A-D-G-B-E

Slowly

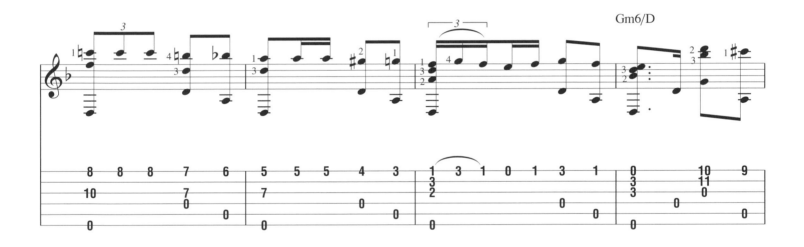

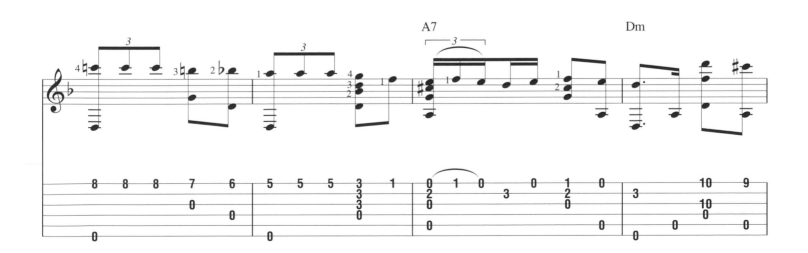

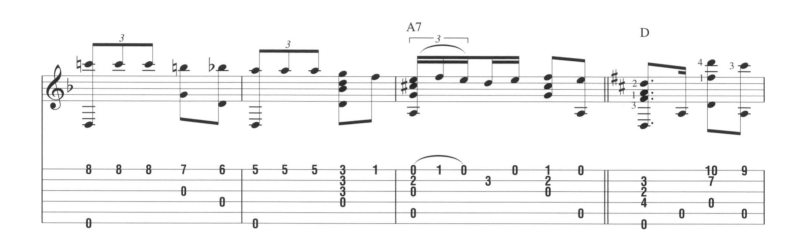

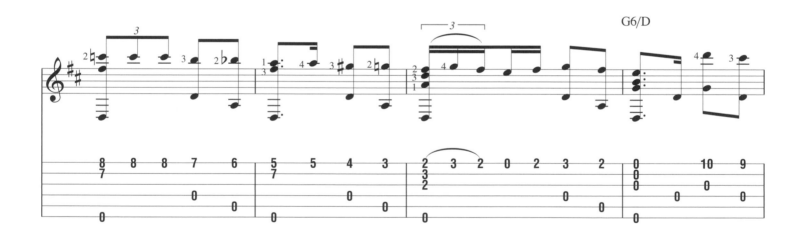

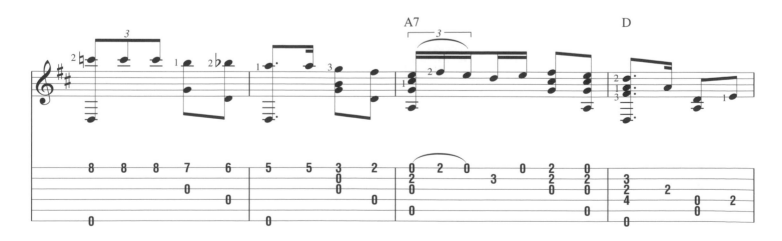

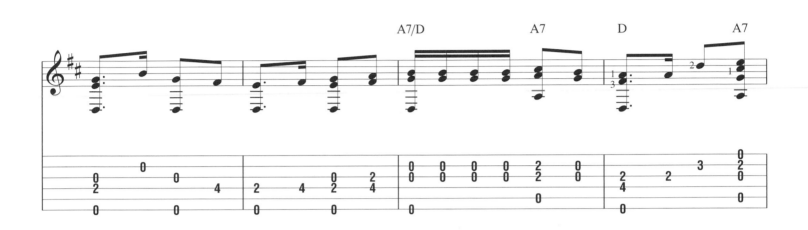

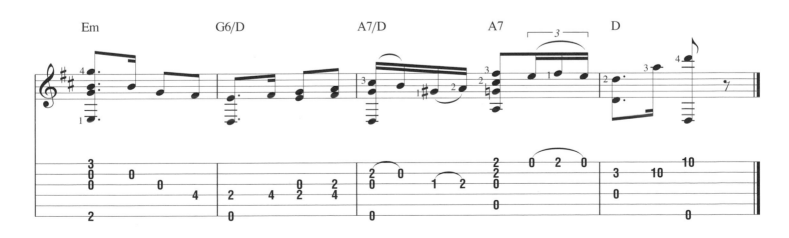

Humoresque

By Antonin Dvorak

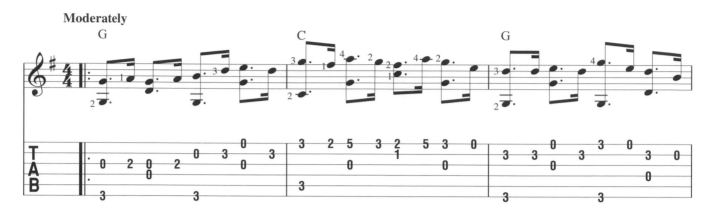

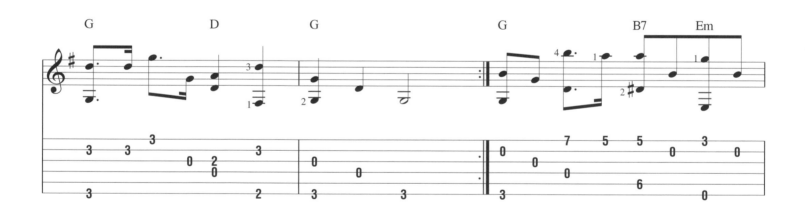

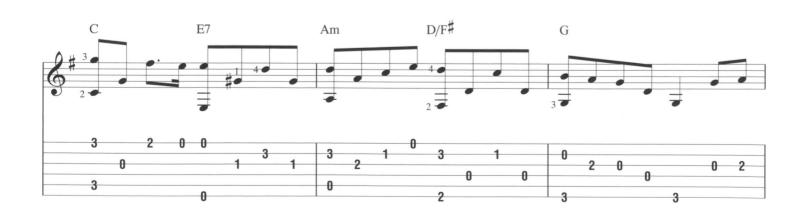

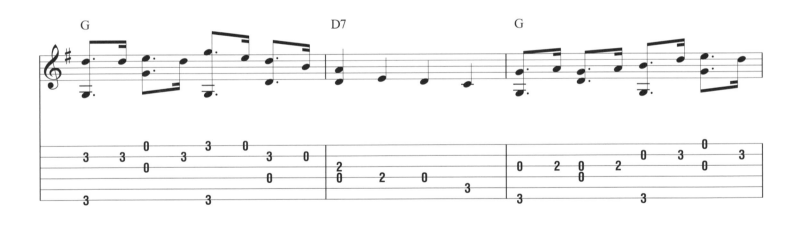

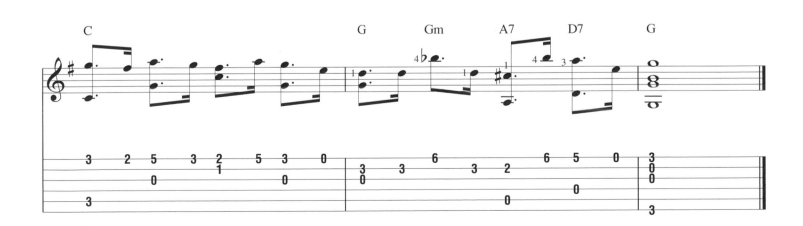

In the Hall of the Mountain King

from PEER GYNT
By Edvard Grieg

Drop D tuning:
(low to high) D-A-D-G-B-E

Moderately

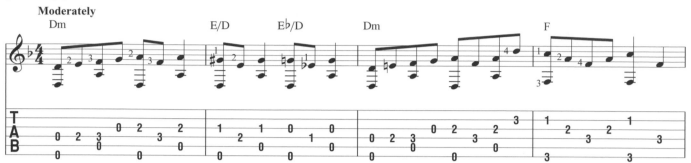

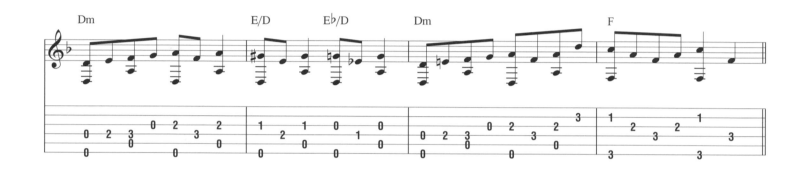

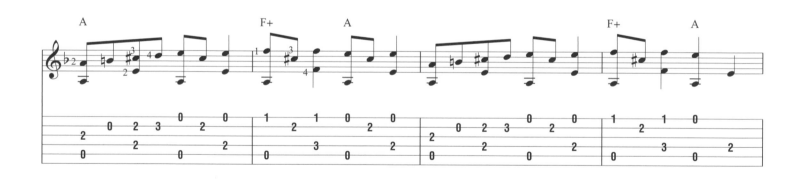

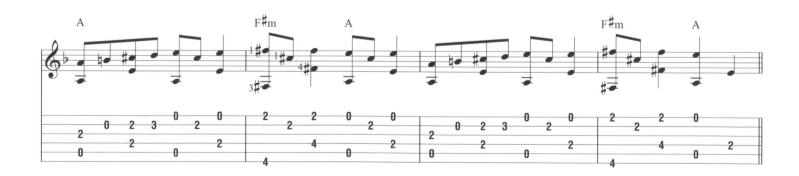

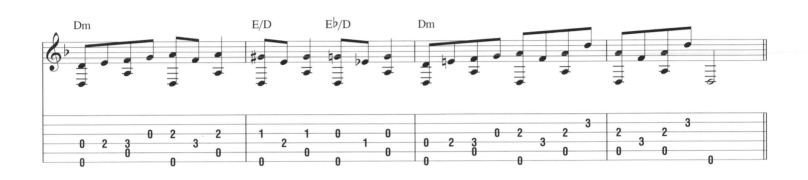

Minuet in G Major

By Johann Sebastian Bach

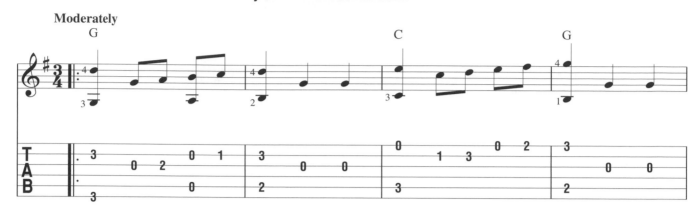

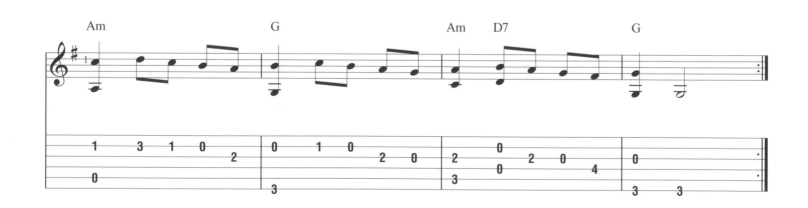

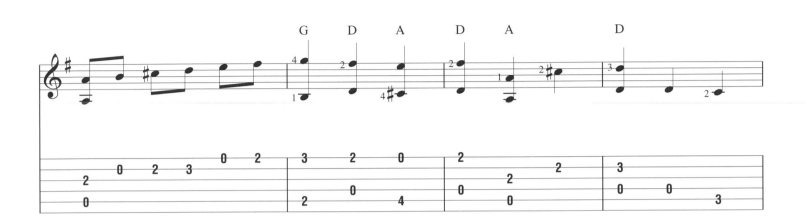

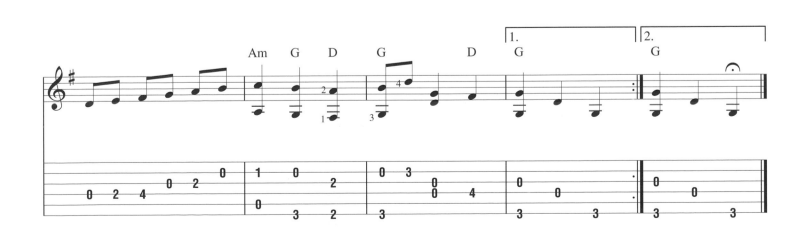

Minuet in G Major

By Ludwig van Beethoven

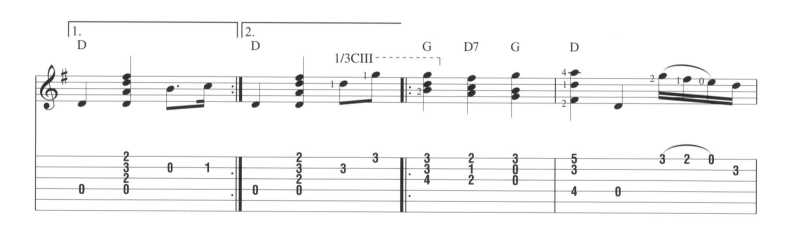

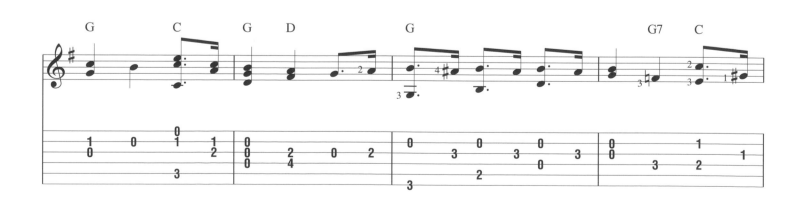

New World Symphony (Theme)

By Antonin Dvorak

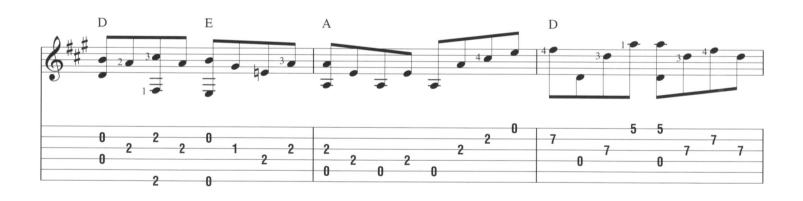

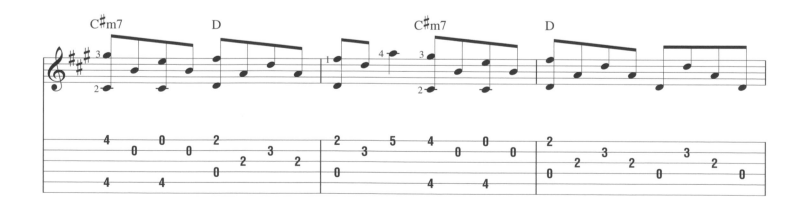

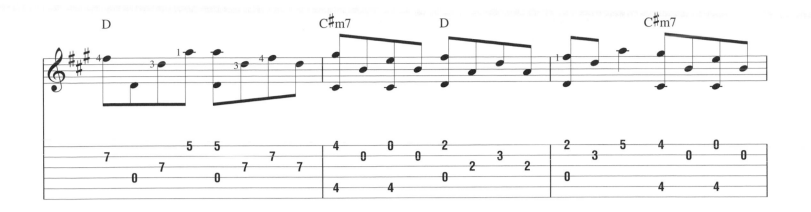

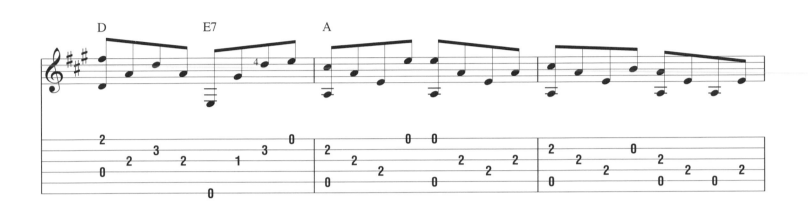

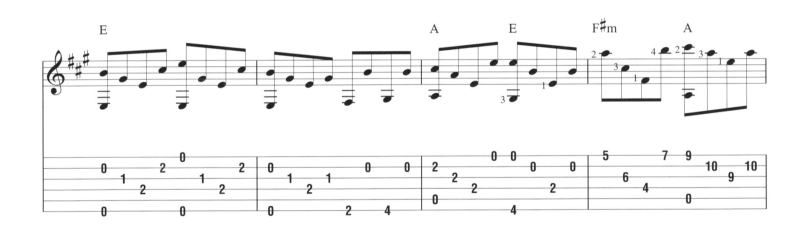

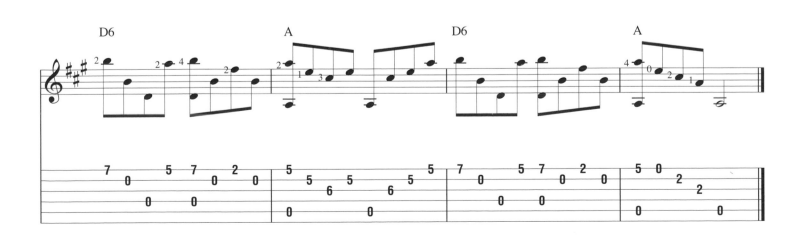

Pomp and Circumstance

Words by Arthur Benson
Music by Edward Elgar

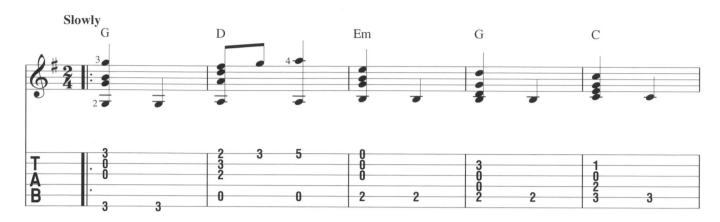

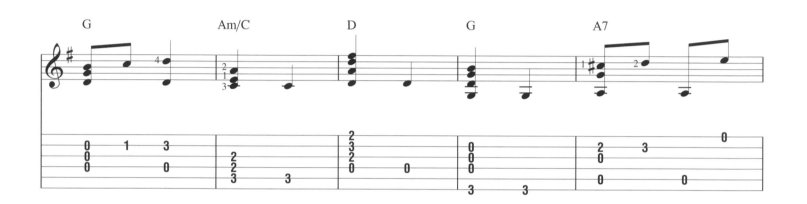

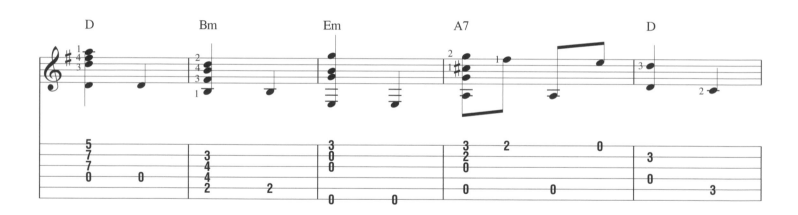

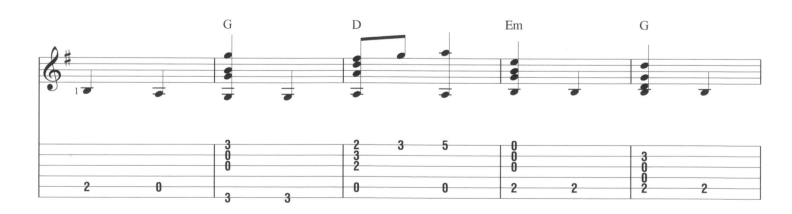

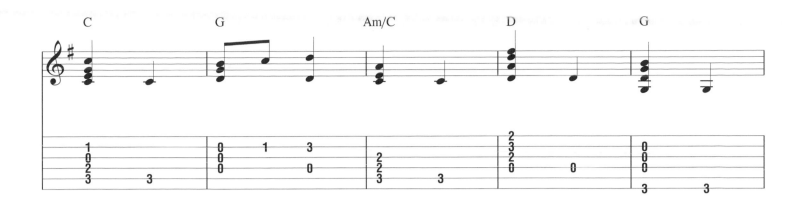

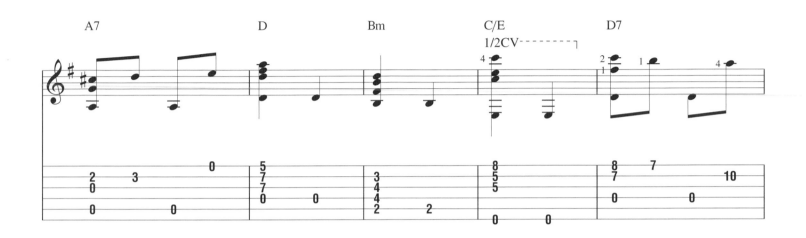

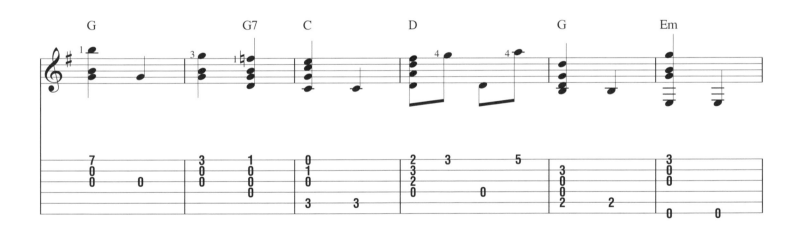

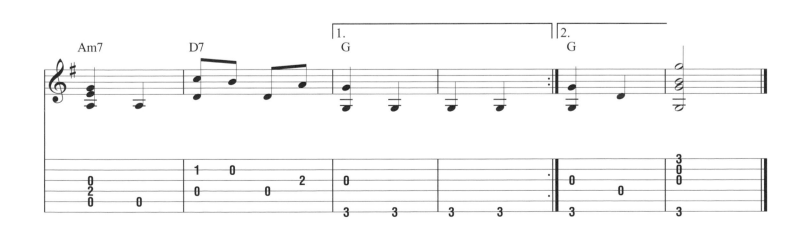

Symphony No. 5 in C Minor, First Movement Excerpt

By Ludwig van Beethoven

*Capo III

Allegro

*This arrangement in A minor for playability.
To play in C minor, capo 3rd fret.